Accept It & Grow

JAMES DANIEL JOHNSON

Copyright © 2015 by James Daniel Johnson.
All rights reserved. No part of this book may be reproduced in any form without written permission from the publisher.

ISBN: 1508564175
ISBN 13: 978-1-5085-6417-1

Acknowledgments

I would like to give special thanks to some of the people who have helped me in life and played a role in inspiring me to write this book.

First, thank you to my mother, Sandra Williams, and to my father, the late James Johnson. As well, thank you to my grandmothers, the late Mary Alice Johnson and the late Ella Mae Green, and my grandfather, Sam Green. Thank you to my aunts, Annie Hairston and Janice Green, my uncles Eugene Johnson, Gerome Johnson, and Jimmy Green. Thank you to my god uncle, the late Jimmy Littles, and my god aunt, Ella Littles. Also, Ms. Jackie Hills, Mr. Anthony Williams, Reverend Ervin Omega Gilliam, my good friends – Henry Johnson, Reuben Malone, Barry Roberts, James Neilson, the late Jerry Mae Watson, and others who have shown me unconditional love!

Thank you to the late Bishop J. H. Shermon. Harold Cushenberry, Gerald Fisher, Ann O'Reagan Keary, Patricia Lewis, Anthony Carter, Samuel Jordan, Frank Marshall, Amadi Boone, Kathleen Fenner, Ronnie Lamb, Dr. John Ndambuki, and Janese Hall. Thank you to Tara and Sarah and the Free Minds Book Club of Washington, DC. Thank you to Nolan, Moye, Jim, Ralph, Hosea, and Chuck of Fed-Ex Kinko's on Tennessee Street in Tallahassee, FL. Thank you to Maria Hampton, Neil Rickard, Eric Falquero, Christine Thomas, John Carney, Marvin Clemons, Bernita Durbin, Freda McDonald, Juanita Wills, and Bruce Simms. Thank you to Mia Batiste, Barbara Garvin, Harmony Rutledge, LaTisha Knight, Laytoya Watson, Michelle Campbell, Sophia Ferraro, Jason Hammer, Rose Rolfe and her daughter Valerie Rolfe. Thank you to Khalil Wiggins, Wise Tarantino, Bill Batts, Reverend Richard Gardner, Tiffany Y. Banks, Miguel Jorge, Jonathan Robinson, Joclyn Carter, Gretchen Rohr, and Bianca Patterson. Thank you to Deloris Mason, Rickey Lewis and The Project Empowerment Program staff of Washington, DC. Thank you to Donald Lee, Ewart Brown, Author Willie Jolley, Roach Brown, Quamiir Trice, Jackie Morgan, Zach Turner,

William Powell, Bernadette V. Collins, and Todd Williams. Thank you to Chris Rix, Robert Contee, Shon Armstrong, Roger Sattler, Apryl Gates, Azim Ross, Demetrius Jackson, Bruce Reid, Cherise Graves, and Leon Holt. Thank you to Michael Caesar, Chaplain Betty Green, Ida Lucas, Ingrid Bergerud, Jeffrey Nelson, Eugene Schneeberg, Michael "Shoemaker" Murray, and the late Ms. Alma Johnson.

Thank you to Shanek Reid for designing the cover of this book; and thank you to Peter Storey for his contribution to the front and back covers.

Thank you to LaFayette Phillips for all of your help. Keep your head in the game.

Thank you to Karl "The Mailman" Malone for the sage advice.

I would also like to thank my best friend, second to Jesus Christ, Donald T. Grafton.

I would like to honor the memory of my beloved godmother, the late Marie L. Bing, who named me when I was born and loved me as if I were her son. She was a genuine God-fearing woman. No doubt she has gone to heaven. Amen.

Finally, I give praise, honor, and glory to my best friend, Jesus Christ, who died for my sins, intercedes for me, and delivers me from the hands of Satan and all others who wish me harm. Jesus has been patient with me. Without him, I would have no hope.

Contents

FAMILY & FRIENDS

He Has A Right 2

His Mind And Heart 4

Inevitably 7

She Was The Definition 9

She Knew 10

Mine Too 12

LOVE

Seriously 14

Where I'm Going 15

What We Have, Not Who We Are 17

She Wanted To Help Us 18

Better Than Burning 19

Too Much 20

ADVICE

One At A Time 22

Literally 23

Why Don't You Care? 24

Cease Supporting Pulpit Pimps 25

Be Your Own Man 27

Priceless Validation 28

Beware 29

Don't Be A Sucker 31

The Wrong Thing 32

You Still Have Time 33

Overlook 35

Pay Attention 36

CHRISTIAN FAITH

Useless 38

Save Myself 39

Stupid And Wrong 40

Consider 41

Just A Test 42

Divine Probation 43

It's Just A Little Sleep 44

It's Coming 45

They Can't See You 46

No Sin 47

Who Am I 48

My Priority 49

MORE FACTS

For Real, Not All 52

It's Only Fair 54

Favor In Your Heart 56

Appropriately 57

Just Faking And Selling Dreams 58

Yes, He Did 60

Simply 61

Just As Good 62

Good Husband, Good Dad 65

Asking For Trouble 66

FAMILY & FRIENDS

He Has A Right

I have endured numerous adversities
Most of which, I am to blame
As well, to my disappointment
My baby brother has experienced much of the same

Although, he's now an adult
I feel responsible in a way
I was a negative example
Which I am embarrassed to say

Yet, for his future I am optimistic
He hasn't given up on himself
He acknowledges his character defects
For his problems, he accuses no one else

Nevertheless, I still feel a bit of guilt
So earnestly, he is in my prayers
I praise the Lord for protecting him
He is being guarded by an angel unaware

The same blood runs through our veins
We're two years and ten months apart
I love Leroy dearly
He has a right to a place in my heart

1 Corinthians 14:20

His Mind And Heart

I have never met my mother's biological father
About this, I have been upset
My opinion of him has been negative
With bitterness, his existence I chose to forget

But, tonight while talking with my mother
He just happened to cross my mind
So, I decided to ask her questions
The facts, I wanted to find

Reluctantly, she told me what happened
Because re-living the past reminds her of pain
She looked directly into my eyes
After all this time, she finally explained

While she was still in the hospital after being born
To go see my mother, he tried
But, on his way to the hospital, he was hit by a car
There on the scene, he died

I'm now ashamed and overwhelmed with guilt
Because his character I wrongly despised
It's also great consolation
And a relief the truth to realize

My grandfather was a decent man
I'm proud that of my family, he is a part
Grandpa didn't intentionally abandon her
When he was killed, my mom was on his mind and in his heart

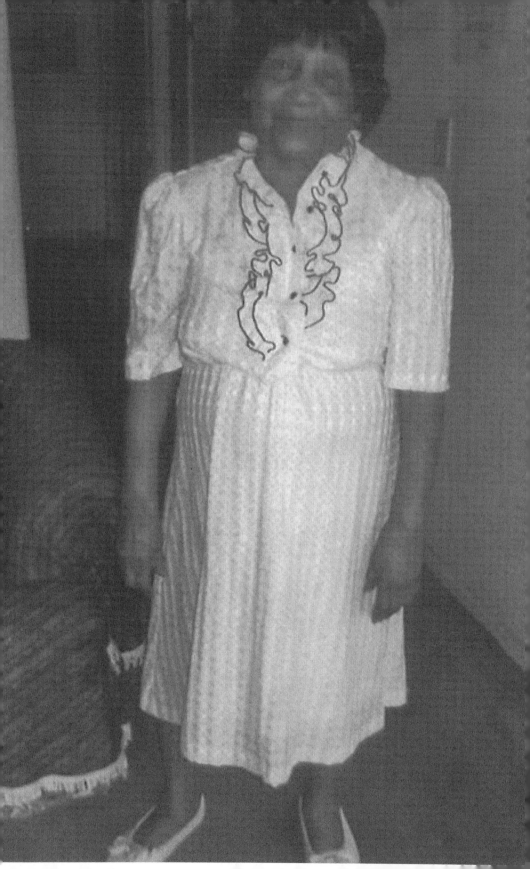

Inevitably

It is three days before Christmas
I'm traveling on an Amtrak train
I'm going to visit my mom
As thoughts of my grandmother captivate my brain

She's recently been admitted to a nursing home
Which causes me grief as well as tears
She is battling diabetes in her old age
She's been around for 90 long years

I now petition God
My hand in prayer up to him I lift
I'm asking Him to further prolong her life
For me, a blessed Christmas gift

However, grandma has said she's tired
To my aunt Annie Lois this she confessed
She told her she's worn out
Prepared to die and get some rest

As I look at it from her perspective
It makes reality a little easier to bear
Especially, because she knows I love her dearly
So much for her I care

For even further consolation
Her eternity is going to be okay
Mary Alice Johnson
Has faith in Jesus, His Word she obeys

In conclusion for me this is also a reminder
To this fact, I'm not dumb
I will also stand before the Lord
For final judgment, inevitably, my date with death will come

She Was The Definition

I now dwell on dear thoughts of Marie L. Bing
It's another one of those days
A reminder to have reverence for God
And gratefully give Him praise

I wish I could bring her back
And repay her for her motherly affection
Yet, it's great consolation that she's resting in peace
As she waits to join Jesus in the resurrection

Her heart was devoted to the Lord
His commandments were her delight
She shunned the evil deeds of darkness
Chose to walk the path of righteous light

Oh how I regret letting her down
My guilt seems to have no end
Besides being my second mother
She was also a real friend

She didn't just go to church on Sundays
With this pen and paper truth I speak
With integrity she lived a Christian life
Seven days a week

Disappointing her motivates my repentance
To publicly honor her memory, I've adamantly begun
If my godmother wasn't a good woman
There never was, nor will ever be one

Revelation 14:13
Proverbs 31:30-31

She Knew

It's January 23, 2015
An unfortunate date
Sad to say, a few hours ago my Aunt Annie Lois,
Informed me that my grandmother died yesterday

I was aware this time was fast approaching,
Her health grew increasingly worse
Medications became useless
And she required personal care from a licensed nurse

As sad as I am over her death
I still have yet to cry
About this, I have questioned myself
And my conscience tells me why

I made amends for breaking her heart
I gave her due reverence and respect
For the past four years, I was determined to give her the honor
She had a right to expect

She is now taking a nap before going to heaven
To miserable mourning, I will not defer
Furthermore, it is consolation to know that
When she died, she knew I loved her

Isaiah 57:1-2
Proverbs 10:7

I DEDICATE THIS POEM TO THE MEMORY
OF MARY ALICE JOHNSON. GOOD BYE
FOR NOW GRANDMA. BY GOD'S GRACE AND
THANKS TO JESUS, I'LL SEE YOU AGAIN
IN HEAVEN, AMEN!!!

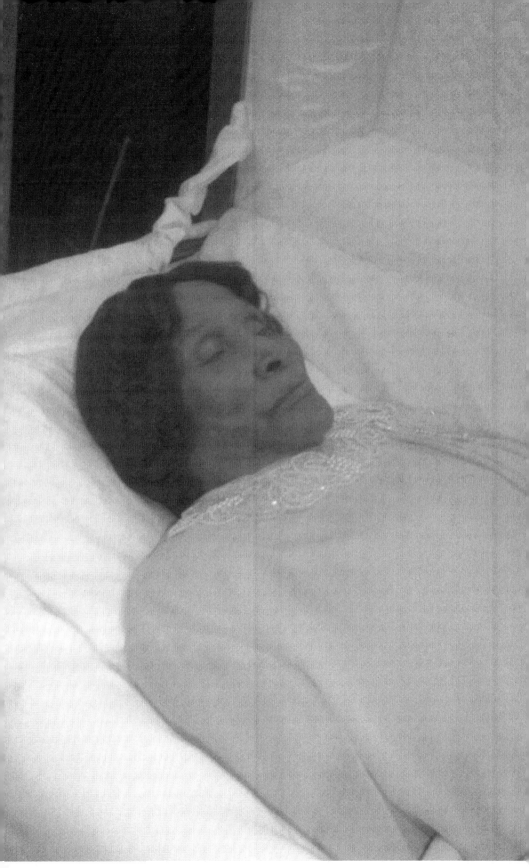

Mine Too

The Bible says there is a friend that sticks closer than a brother
From experience, I know this to be true
Derrick kept it real
No matter what I was going through

December 15, 2014
Death knocked on my best friend's door
He breathed his last breath
Of this life his part was no more

When I heard the news, I was devastated
His demise I refused to believe
While shocked I shed many tears
Forever by this I am grieved

Big "D" was a gentle giant
A heart of gold he possessed
His friendship I consider priceless
A fact I'm blessed to profess

I'm obligated to honor his memory
Derrick, I miss you, rest in peace
I pray to someday see you in heaven
Eventually, my earthly life too will cease

Proverbs 18:24
Revelation 13:14
Hebrews 9:27

LOVE

Seriously

Women are so unpredictable
Just when you think you know them, you realize you don't
From experience, I know this to be true
I want to deny it, but I won't

Several times, I've been dumped
Once to hold back my tears, I had to fight
They told me I was doing a lot of wrong
But, I thought I was doing everything right

Once again, I'm single in search for love
I desire commitment for life
I'm looking for a healthy, God fearing woman
That wants to be my wife

There are a few who have captured my attention
Yet, wisely I must pursue
I should be cautious and not overconfident
Due to disappointments I've been through

Women are like alien crossword puzzles
Impossible to figure out
Nevertheless, I will try
But, to succeed, I seriously doubt

Philippians 4:6-7

Where I'm Going

Time after time, I've experienced rejection
Indeed emotionally rough
Women I desire deny me a chance
Because they think for them I'm not good enough

Addiction and incarceration
Were once all that I knew
Alcohol and drugs both held me captive
The sea of self-destruction I swam through

However, today redemption is mine
I'm highly favored as well as blessed
Finally using the potential the Lord gave me
I'm traveling the road to success

Therefore, I refuse to be discouraged
With faith I claim the woman of my dreams
Those who arrogantly rejected me
Have only fueled my self-esteem

As far as I'm concerned it's their loss
Confidently all doubt away I'm throwing
I'm not interested in any women who judges me by where I've been
But, in one who loves and wants me for where I'm going

Isaiah 43:18-19
Jeremiah 29:11-13

What We Have, Not Who We Are

A lot of women label us as "dogs"
An unequal stigma placed on "real men"
To address the fact of this matter
It is time to begin

Some women are "dogs" too
They can't be trusted and love to cheat
Prolific manipulators, they claim integrity
But are full of deceit

They say from their man, they want love
And loyalty, to them this is what matters most
However, it's just another of their lies
Without shame they emphatically boast

Many women today are materialistic
"Gold-diggers" ever so smart
In actuality, she's the pimp
It's a joke for her to break your heart

Men stop being "suckers" thinking you're Mr. Cool
When a woman of this character plays you
With much regret
You'll feel like a fool

So, if ever unfortunately you experience this
Don't be angry with anyone else
Instead of blaming her for your stupidity
You should blame yourself

Pay close attention to her heart and not only her booty
Do yourself a favor and be wise
Some women are daughters of the devil
By their beauty well disguised

This is indeed a fact
From reality don't be far
The majority of women want men
For what they have, not who we are

She Wanted To Help Us

For quite some time, I've been writing poetry
But, I've never written one about her
Suddenly, I'm consumed with guilt
Deserved regret does occur

Like several other women who truly loved me
Of them, Michelle was one
When we began our relationship
I said to take her place there was none

She had two babies by some other brother
10 months was the boy and 2 years old her little girl
I loved them as if they were my own
To me, they meant the world

Besides being a natural beauty
Michelle had integrity in her heart
She applied for a job and was hired
With the bills, she wanted to do her part

But, I wouldn't let her take the job
I was working and had a honest hustle on the side
I thought by myself I could handle it
For her and the kids provide

Gradually, our bills got too steep
We began to argue day and night
My ego wouldn't allow me to admit I was wrong
In her complaints, she indeed was right

Soon after, we broke up
Yet, 20 years later with myself I fuss
I tried to do too much
And prevented Michelle from helping us

Better Than Burning

As a Christian, I have an obligation
I must humbly practice self-control
If I don't grace won't save me
In hell, I'll lose my soul

Many other Christians disagree
John 3:16 is often misunderstood
Yet, about this I'm no longer confused
Needless to say, for my own good

I can't continue to intentionally sin
Taking for granted God's grace
Hebrews 10:26-31 confirms
The fact I've begun to face

I yearn for a beautiful God fearing wife
Day after day, I'm overwhelmed with lust
But 1 Corinthians 9:24-27
Explains self-discipline is a must

Sex is indeed pleasurable
But, only condoned by God when it's husband with his wife
Hebrews 13:2 is a stern warning
In the Book that guides us to eternal life

So, patience is a necessity
The woman of my dreams with faith I claim
When we're married we can make love
God won't be angry and we'll bear no shame

Along with me please be convinced
From this poem a lesson learn
Do yourself a favor
And accept the fact that it's better to marry than to burn

1 Corinthians 7:1-9
Romans 1:18-32

Too Much

If I said I've fallen in love with you
That would be a lie
Yet, for me it seems like love at first sight
A fact I can't deny

To express what I feel words would fail
A disappointment indeed
I've been a slave to wishful thinking
From the world of fantasy, it's time to be freed

At least take this heart
I say this without exaggeration
Your natural beauty amazes me
Beyond your imagination

I apologize if I seem excessively persistent
The thought of annoying you is something I hate
Lack of patience is a sin
Good things come to those who wait

If we're meant to be it will happen
This manifestation I long for much
Dorrelle, I've acknowledged the fact
That perhaps from you I want too much

ADVICE

One At A Time

We all want good health and long life
So, it's important to stay in shape
Yet, some refuse to eat properly and exercise
From logic they wish to escape

They love foods that aren't good for them
Always have an excuse not to work out
The regret they will eventually suffer
To actually occur they doubt

To address their lack of concern
They need motivation
Stop taking life for granted
And change their thinking with determination

Start drinking a lot of water
Reduce salt and sugar in their diet
This simple adjustment will prevent illness
And save their bodies an internal riot

Noticeable results won't happen over night
But, gradually with persistence satisfaction you'll find
You can drastically improve your physical fitness
And it's done one day at a time

1 Timothy 4:6-8

Literally!

I just don't understand it
To help us Oh Lord, I pray
African Americans are so far behind
Though we've come a long way

We claim to love one another
We'll adamantly profess this to be fact
Yet, we are our own worst enemies
Stabbing ourselves in the back

We won't support our own black businesses
A shameful reality we want to ignore
While foreigners monopolize our neighborhoods
We would rather spend our money in their stores

Many of our youth lack proper guidance
Overwhelmed by their communities negative persuasion
They have no reverence for the Lord, not to mention their parents
And fail to value the worth of essential education

Instead of us sincerely uniting to make things better
We fake like together we stand
Some of our black leaders are merely "house niggers"
With selfish ambitions and political plans

It is time to stop blaming the "white man" for all our problems
How long the evident will we deny
A lot of white folk actually love us
They've proved it in the past and in the present still try

Today, we are responsible for many of our problems
Let's take a honest look at self
Though some racial discrimination still exist
We are literally enslaving ourselves

Proverbs 3:5-6

Why Don't You Care?

If you are a parent
You have a serious obligation
You must provide for your child
Without inexcusable procrastination

Unfortunately, some parents are taken for granted
Which isn't fair as well as rude
Their children are disrespectful
And show them no gratitude

A hard headed and stubborn child
Causes grief and shame
For the consequences of their foolish behavior
Instead of themselves their parents they blame

These children laugh at good advice
To them wisdom is a joke
They become annoying
The anger of their parents they provoke

So, if you're a mother or father
To you this fact, I'm inspired to reveal
If you claim to be a child of God
Why do you deliberately disrespect Him with no regard for how He feels?

John 8:34-47

Cease Supporting Pulpit Pimps

Demonic spirits have infiltrated most churches
Trying to imitate God's voice
The congregations are being misled
Some ignorantly, some by choice

The scenario of choice is for real
For God many have no fear
They choose to attend churches that condone their sinful life styles
And feast on the lies they prefer to hear

Phony preachers are on the rise
Accumulating fortune and fame
Devils well disguised
Selfish agendas fuel their game

Their sermons distort the meaning of the Lord's grace
Biblical truth they prolifically dilute
Boldly defending their erroneous doctrines
In them God's Word has no root

These religious entertainers are masters of flattery
Both male and female
Their words are so persuasive
They can dive in the ocean and sell more water to a whale

Be a wise soldier for Jesus Christ
Stand loyal in the faith and don't be a wimp
Have no association with false prophets
Cease supporting these pulpit pimps

2 Corinthians 11:13-15
Deuteronomy 18:18
Matthew 23:23-28

Be Your Own Man

The minds of the youth are being poisoned
Due to lack of guidance, they are being misled
Peer pressure fuels this fire
Which I think need not be said

It's especially worse with boys
To be tough and cool they are compelled to show
An epidemic of psychological cancer
That is more common in the projects and ghetto

Drugs and violence are the chief culprits
Their victims so much they hate
These two demons are far from racist
They do not discriminate

Millions of lives they've destroyed
The numbers are hard to believe
You would think by now the problem would be resolved
Yet, both continue to ruin as well as deceive

I now pray for all youth caught up in this web
And earnestly for those who are male
Because they are the primary targets of this destruction
Confirmations are funerals and the population in jail

Young men let go of foolishness
Wisdom from above, seek and understand
Abstain from negativity and have reverence for the Lord
Don't follow the crowd, be your own man

Joshua 24:14-15
Psalm 119:9-16
Psalm 1:1-3

Priceless Validation

I'm engrossed with inspiration
This opportunity I appreciate
I'm obligated to enlighten
It's a privilege to elaborate

I have wasted so much of my life
Desiring others to exalt me
Trying to impress them
Became my supreme priority

From that foolishness I've been released
This destructive burden has been laid to rest
As long as I am obeying the commandments of God
What you think of me I could care less

Many more are enslaved by the need to impress
Their time and energy they give a lot
Furthermore, they will proudly deny it
But, oh so true, believe it or not

If this shoe fits, you wake up
In your heart permit pure wisdom to dwell
The folks from whom you yearn praise
Don't own the keys to heaven and hell

Sincerely crave the approval of the Lord
Let it be your number one aspiration
Reject the influence of demonic spirits
Only from Jesus do you need validation

John 12:37-43
2 Corinthians 10:17-18

Beware

The wounds of a friend are faithful
Kisses from an enemy are full of deceit
It is futile to fight biblical advice
God's Word, no one can defeat

Accepting facts sometimes hurts
So, reality many choose to ignore
People who hate correction themselves
Tell lies like rain pours

It's an epidemic fueled by pride
Which has been around for so long
They claim they are right
And deny ever being wrong

These individuals are slaves of flattery
Self-ambition well they know
They enjoy the company of anyone
Who will stroke their ego

Indeed it is a two way street
Consider what you are reading dear
Beware of people who love to be told
As well as tell others what they want to hear

Proverbs 26:28
Proverbs 27:5-6

Don't Be A Sucker

Just moments ago, I was wrongfully humiliated
By Kaneisha, I was misled
She was playing me with malicious intentions
The thought of her deceit never entered my head

With disappointment, I was shocked
Indeed a rude surprise
She now reminds me of Jezebel
A woman whom God despised

After a misunderstanding, she accepted my apology
And my hopes she continued to deliberately lift
Three days ago when I went to visit her
She asked me to go buy her some flowers or a gift

Today, when I stopped by to say hi
I felt like crying a pool of water
Her supervisor said against me
Kaneisha was planning to file a restraining order

Hard to believe she's so insidious to prove I adored her
She knew I was zealous
She used me to get attention from her co-workers
And to make another man jealous

The Bible provides warnings about such women
Instructs a man how to correctly live
So, sincerely I wish her well
Her deception, I forgive

Oh, what a valuable lesson I've learned
To share this experience, I consider my duty
Gentlemen, beware of a smooth talking woman
Don't be a sucker for her beauty

Genesis 39:1-20
Proverbs 6:23-26
Proverbs 31:1-3
Ecclesiastes 7:26

The Wrong Thing

Due to some unfortunate circumstances
I have been a slave to low self-esteem
Yet, by the grace of God
From this bondage, I have been redeemed

I once sought other people's approval
A compulsion, I have finally addressed
A fact I am no longer
Ashamed to confess

My priorities have been out of place
The truth I have accepted and believe
A relief to overcome the demonic spirits
By which I have been deceived

Today, I'm experiencing desired peace
In my heart, serenity dwells
It is my duty to please God, not man
I want to go to heaven, not hell

These words are to encourage and enlighten
Intended to set many free
I'm compelled to write this poem for you
And needless to say, for me

In all you say and do seek to please God
To your attention wisdom I bring
If you are choosing the praise of people before the praise of God
You are worrying about the wrong thing

John 12:37-43

You Still Have Time

Satan is not a myth
He's the king demon and father of lies
To convince people he doesn't really exist
Cunningly, he tries

His goal is to keep us from turning to Jesus
He'll do anything possible to create your doubt
Those who he can beguile will be even more miserable
When too late the truth they find out

He attacks our minds
Our focus is top objective
Causing distraction is a part of his arsenal
To his schemes, he doesn't want us perceptive

What comes before reverence for the commandments of Jesus Christ?
Is the Lord not first in your heart?
Failure to love and obey Him
Is not smart

Rejecting Jesus is detrimental
In the eyes of God, a heinous crime
If you're reading this poem, all hope isn't lost
To grasp your greatest priority by grace you still have time

2 Peter 3:1-9
Romans 2:4-11

Overlook

Some people possess a malicious character
Of life an unfortunate part
They pretend to be a good person
However, wickedness consumes their heart

They slander and insult others
But, when you confront them about it, they'll deny
Then laugh and make jokes about it
As they love to tell a lie

These kinds of people, you must learn to ignore
Like them, don't be the same
Eventually, the Lord will hold them accountable
For their insidious games

So, let God do His job
In your frustration, stay cool
Never do evil for evil
In your heart allow humility to rule

Strive to do what is right
God will surely reward you some day
When children of the devil insult you and assassinate your character
Be meek and overlook what they say

Proverbs 12:16
1 Peter 2:19-23

Pay Attention

None of us are without sin
When it comes to doing wrong, we all have done our share
Some of us acknowledge our faults and strive to change
While some love evil and just don't care

To everyone who will read or hear this poem
Consider which category you are in
If you're one of those who think hell is just a myth
I advise you to think again

The devil has blinded the minds of many people
To accept Jesus into their heart they stubbornly refuse
With no regard for the life after death
Eternal agony they choose

To deceive, Satan has fathered various religions
Which the Bible warned us that he would
However, he knows he can't trick us all
Though, viciously, he wishes he could

The lake of fire is his future
His fate without hope is sealed
It's hard to believe how many seem to love him
Especially, since he hates them for real

Wake up and be wise
Repentance will ensure your damnation prevention
Jesus died on the cross to save you
Give Him your heart, to this warning pay attention

Proverbs 29:1

CHRISTIAN FAITH

Useless

God speaks to us in various ways
To deliver us from darkness to the light
I believe one is a song sung by Prince
"Money Don't Matter Tonight"

I totally agree with the songs message
To me the point got across
Instead of focusing on material possessions
I should ensure my soul isn't lost

It's obvious that many don't get the meaning
Maybe they do, but just don't care
Which is indeed insanity because of
Consequences they've been made aware

Little do they know that they've sold
Their souls to the devil
They've taken the definition of foolish
To its highest possible level

Ungrateful and full of greed
Love for the Lord they disregard
To get to heaven they think they can
Write a check or swipe a credit card

God doesn't accept bribes
Tickets to His kingdom, he doesn't sell
By the way, you should also know
That money is useless in hell

Luke 16:19-31

Save Myself

I often write about faith in Jesus
The son of God and Prince of Peace
I'm compelled to witness about the Lord
So others won't share the doomed fate of the evil beast

Yet, the Bible gives this great emphasis
A stern warning to all that teach
We too must obey the scriptures
It is mandatory that we practice what we preach

Here, I sit in conviction
To renounce excuses it's time to begin
My faith in Jesus has been hypocritical
Because I have intentionally committed sins

However, the Lord has shown me pity
Although, my disrespect no doubt He resents
With me, He is being gentle
Empowering me to sincerely repent

I will continue my ministry
Which is surely going to save someone else
As well, I'm determined to overcome temptation
Obey God's Word and save myself

Romans 2:21-24
1 Timothy 4:12-16
1 Corinthians 9:24-27

Stupid And Wrong

Some people don't have common sense
While a baby, on their heads they must have been dropped
They seem so intelligent
But their elevator doesn't go all the way to the top

They have no reverence for God
Preferring to live without Him they think is okay
Yet, when they get into a precarious situation
They suddenly want to pray

As well, when death comes for such a person
From family and friends, you'll hear hypocritical cries
During their funeral service in a church
On their behalf, the preacher will tell lies

To get the point across, I'm being blunt
I hope you can take a hint
It is wise to have faith in God
And also sincerely repent

In your choices be mature
Or you will sing the misery song
To insult God and expect Him to save you
Is stupid as well as wrong

Hebrews 10:23-31
Proverbs 19:3

Consider

It's a privilege to give God the glory
To Him all praise belongs
Because of His gentleness, I'm living better days
And singing the redemption song

I've beaten the demons of alcohol and drugs
The cost of misery, I no longer pay
But, I remember those whom the Lord used
To help me along the way

Some bought me food when I was hungry
And really needed to eat
Some bought me clothes and
A decent pair of shoes to wear on my feet

Some gave me shelter
Unemployed and homeless, I couldn't pay rent
Some gave me priceless advice
And much needed encouragement

Some were black, some were white
Some from other races and creeds
If God used my addiction to help me overcome racism
He did succeed

I thank God for them all
Of my testimony they are a part
I pray the Lord reward them for the compassion
In their hearts

To formally acknowledge the individuals
I've just described is the least I could do
If by chance, of them, you are one
Consider this poem just for you

Matthew 5:7
Matthew 25:31-46

Just A Test

Job was indeed a good man
His story the Bible does tell
Although, he had reverence for God
Still during his life he experienced some hell

He did nothing to deserve his calamities
Which seems unfair as well as odd
The devil devised a plan to destroy Job
And give him reason to curse God

However, Job maintained his integrity
All his troubles did he humbly endure
He refused to foolishly disrespect the omnipotent
Job loved the Lord because his heart was pure

The scheme of Satan failed
Job confirmed his faith was strong
Again, like He always will
God beat the devil and proved him wrong

So, if you are suffering because of your faith in Jesus
It doesn't mean you haven't done something right
The devil is trying to persuade you to curse God
Understand you are in a spiritual fight

Whenever Satan causes you adversity
Your loyalty to the Lord will surely be blessed
Don't succumb to the attack of the father of lies
It is just your faith being put to the test

Job 42:1-17

Divine Probation

I know the Bible better than most
In Jesus Christ, I believe
I understand the meaning of His grace
In this matter, I am not deceived

Some people think that grace is a license to sin
They have no regard for its abuse
Yet, for their ignorance in this matter
The Lord will grant them no excuse

I've overcome numerous sins
But, struggle with some still
I'm not obeying the Lord the way that I should
With myself, I must keep it real

The Bible makes it very clear
In the trap of deception don't fall
I've been following God with part of my heart
But to please Him, I must follow with all

Sad to say many churches are being misled
The clergy aren't teaching what is true
Congregations prefer to hear sermons that compromise God's Word
So, they justify the transgressions they love to do

I don't want my name erased from the Book of Life
My priority is seeking salvation
I've been insulting God's patience
I realize, I'm on Divine Probation

Psalm 103:10-11

It's Just A Little Sleep

It is Sunday morning and I am sitting in church
Falling asleep, I fight
Because of unfortunate circumstances
I only got two hours of rest last night

6 AM, I finally got in bed
Reluctantly, I woke up at eight
When I'm tired, I feel miserable
I have a short fuse and am easy for others to irritate

Yet, when it comes to praising God and attending church
I'm compelled to persevere
Being tired isn't an excuse
Because the Lord to me has been so dear

I recall when I was an alcoholic
And smoking crack
I often wouldn't sleep for four or five days
Perhaps hard to believe, but it is a fact

So, missing sleep should never stop me from going to church
To remember this truth, I must never forget
God has given me favor that I don't deserve
I am forever in His debt

I've lived a foolish life
By God's grace, I am not dead
It's a blessing to be in church this morning
After praising God, I'm going home to get back in bed

Hebrews 10:24-25

It's Coming

There are two kinds of wisdom
One is Earthly and the other from above
If you possess the latter you fear God
Your obedience to Him, he counts as love

But, if you boast about Earthly wisdom
Sad to say, you're being deceived
You fail to realize that faith in Jesus is essential
So, that with you, God will be pleased

This faith requires repentance
Premeditated sin you must erase
Don't misunderstand faith in Jesus, if you're rebellious
And intentionally sin, then you are abusing God's grace

The penalty for this, God has made clear
To dispute with integrity, no one can
Read Hebrews chapter 10 verses 26 to 31
So, that you will understand

Beware of the lustful pleasures of this world
To allow them to rule you be advised to never
The sins you enjoy are a one way ticket to hell
Which is the holding cell of torment forever

Cease to think of fun you can have now
Address the issue that is far greater
It's in your best interest to escape eternal damnation
Because, for so many it is coming later

Romans 2:4-11
James 3:13-18

They Can't See

Chilling out at Chinatown Metro Station
Northwest, Washington, DC
I'm suddenly inspired to express my thoughts
While thanking God for all He's done for me

It is evident this world is drastically changing
Overall, reverence for Jesus is lost
People worship their own agendas
Little do they know, the devil has become their boss

Moral principles are on the decline
Insidious deeds folks use to succeed
It's so hard to trust those you think that you can
Because of their evil ambitions and greed

Yes, it's really sad
Unfortunately, oh so true
Furthermore, it's going to get worse
As demonic spirits do what they do

Our disregard for the Lord is the problem
We must answer to Him above all else
Ignorantly, most people are rejecting the Bible
Because it makes them honestly look at themselves

Stop following the crowd and prepare for your own eternity
Understand that Jesus is the one you'll be wise to please
Satan's deception is seductive destruction
His victims can't see the forest for the trees

2 Timothy 2:22-26
Romans 1:18-32

No Sin

I'm at war with the devil
Against me, his demons fight
I'm an anointed vessel of the Lord
Struggling with wrong as I desire to do right

Lust for beautiful women
And resentment to name a few
Wanting revenge and using profanity
To my shame are things I do

As a believer in Jesus Christ, I have an obligation
I must maintain self-control
This issue a lot of Christians disregard
And if they continue, it will cost them their souls

Needless to say, this includes me
As I now admonish myself, I teach
It's impossible for me to be accepted into heaven
Unless I practice what I preach

I must cease succumbing to temptation
Sin, I have to resist
To follow the Lord with all my heart
Is first on my priority list

No doubt, I'm a threat to Satan
He doesn't want the truth exposed
The Lord has given me the gift to preach the gospel
A fact the devil knows

He now comes against me with the weapon of slander
My character, he viciously attacks
I shouldn't resent the people he uses to do this
Overlook their insults and in anger not act

Being a Christian isn't always easy
A better man, I strive to be
God wants me to come to the point
Where no sin has rule over me

Who Am I?

Both my character and intelligence were just again insulted
Yet, on my temper I have a firm grip
Safe to say, in a positive way
On my shoulder, I'm carrying a chip

My faith belongs to Jesus Christ
Which I adamantly profess without hesitation
So, when I encounter individuals who speak evil of me
To be more humble becomes my motivation

The only mediator between God and man was perfect
Christ never did any wrong
He endured envious liars
Such abuse to Him was a common song

He did not resort to revenge
He chose not to retaliate
For His believers, He set an example
Showing love to His enemies instead of hate

This truth gives me strength
Heavenly wisdom I dare not deny
They had the nerve to slander the Prince of Peace
Therefore, to complain, who am I?

Proverbs 19:11
1 Peter 2:19-23
Psalm 37:7-13

My Priority

I was cross-eyed for a while as a child
In elementary school, I was often teased
This upset my godmother
She was very displeased

She asked a doctor if the problem could be fixed
She sympathized with my frustration
She saved up her hard earned money
To help pay for my operation

Although, my surgery was successful
The emotional scars failed to heal
Several years later, I experienced abuse
An attribute to low self-esteem within, I denied to feel

I became focused on the opinion of others
The approval of many was my goal
It practically became an obsession
A war in my mind, hell on Earth to my soul

Thankfully, I have overcome this vicious obstacle
No doubt by divine grace
Today, I'm much older and a little wiser
What counts the most I can finally face

The opinion of God is the greatest
On that great of judgment, only He can condemn
I've had enough of dwelling on what others think about me
My priority is to focus on Him

Hebrews 3:1

MORE FACTS...

For Real – Not All

The racist/criminal violence of law enforcement officers has
Devastated families and taken a priceless life
As well, it has provoked anger
Further fueling hatred and strife

By this harsh reality, I'm grieved
My emotions mere words can't possibly tell
Nevertheless, I attempt as I write
To at least try I am compelled

I've had some encounters with police
Because on drugs, I was hooked
Praise God, today I've overcome that demon
By grace my brain wasn't cooked

I crossed paths with cops who were evil
They took corruption to another level
Although hired to serve with integrity
It's obvious that they work for the devil

I've also crossed paths with cops that have reverence for God
No doubt their conscience the Lord does guide
With integrity they do their jobs,
Respect for their fellow man in their heart abides

Some cops tried to help me when I was homeless
They showed genuine sympathy for my downfall
But, some fabricated arrest reports
And beat me up when I was handcuffed for no reason at all

So, with these facts in mind
I would be wrong to deny what's true
It's not fair to blame the honest cops
For what the dirty ones do

(CONTINUED FROM PREVIOUS PAGE)

Wicked police are a disgrace to their profession
Pretending to be righteous, they have the nerve
Eventually, God will judge them
And repay them what they deserve

The abuse of the badge is out of control
Brothers and sisters, we should be mad
Yet, in conclusion, from personal experience
I can sincerely say all cops aren't bad

Acts 10:1-35
Proverbs 22:22-23

I DEDICATE THIS POEM
TO THE LAW ENFORCEMENT OFFICERS
THAT HAVE A CONSCIENCE
AND REVERANCE FOR ALMIGHTY GOD.

It's Only Fair

Brothers and sisters, please hear me out
This is something I have to say
This matter provokes my concern
I'm beginning to feel some type of way

We were put on ships and transported from Africa
Our beloved motherland
After all of our harsh suffering
Your resentments, I can understand

But let's deal with the facts
Stop being blind to what should be seen
A lot of God fearing white folks despised our mistreatment
To get us justice they intervened

They were scrutinized and threatened
With moral integrity they endured the strife
Some, in our defense
Even lost their life

It's because of their support things have drastically changed
Our equal rights, they weren't afraid to address
For them, I'm truly grateful
Their intervention was a success

Brothers and sisters, let's think maturely
In the face of reality stare
Acknowledge that many white folks love and respect us
This is only fair

Proverbs 3:27
John 7:24
1 Samuel 16:7

Favor In Your Heart

I'm proof that God is plentiful in mercy
Failing to proclaim it, I don't have the nerve
The kindness He's continuously shown me
I realize I don't deserve

My sins are many
Some I committed out of my mind
The eyes of the Lord are everywhere
He's seen it all, to none is He blind

Because of His patience, I'm not destroyed
I could never have a better friend
In His anger He's been gentle with me
My hope for the future hasn't come to an end

He has used special people
To further convince me that He exists
For a fact
You are one at the top of that list

You had the authority to be harsh
Yet, chose to restrain
Soon after, I disappointed you
So, I'm determined to confirm your pity for me wasn't in vain

Words can't express my gratitude
Nevertheless, I'm obligated to start
Judge "C," you could have dogged me out
I praise God for granting me favor in your heart

Daniel 1:9

Appropriately

In life, communication is essential
For healthy relationships, it's the key
Unfortunately, the hard way
Many will come to see

Pride, shame, and dishonesty
In this matter play major roles
Characteristics influenced by the devil
To help him claim more souls

It's the cause of grudges
Hate and wars are deadly obstacles to mankind
The resolution is quite simple
But, by deceit it blinds the mind

The combination of respect and understanding is priceless
Together they are harmonious twins
When joined with love they become blessings
And keep you from intentional sins

I encourage you to remember these words
I'm compelled to get this off my chest
The world would be a better place
If our emotions we would all learn to appropriately express

Ephesians 4:26-27

Just Faking And Selling Dreams

In my pursuit to become a successful author
I've encountered obstacles I thought I never would
I've met numerous people who've promised to help me
But, they've proven their word is no good

Here, I sit disappointed again
To count on them I was persuaded for sure
I'm now at war with bitterness and resentment
For relief, I must pray, it's the only cure

I'm not bragging, but I know the value of my talent
All I need is promotion to soar
It is evident without exposure
My books will be ignored

Nevertheless, I will persevere
To give up, I refuse
My true help comes from the Lord
With Him, I can't lose

My success, God has ordained
Regardless of those who lie to me and scheme
They feel no shame for their lack of integrity
I had to learn, some people are just faking and selling dreams

Proverbs 25:19

Yes, He Did

On November 23, 2014
He breathed his last breath
The best mayor in the history of Washington, DC
Took his turn at the taste of death

Nevertheless, his legacy still lives
And die it will never
He helped so many less fortunate people
Make their lives better

Like every one of us, he wasn't perfect
A truth no one needs to fight
Yet, he asked God for forgiveness
Repented and did what was right

He was a soldier for equal justice
Another reason I'm one of his fans
He stood up for his people
He was proud to be a black man

He wasn't arrogant
A fact no one should ignore
He was a powerful man with a humble spirit
Who reached out to the homeless and the poor

Needless to say, I'm going to miss him
Until I too meet my end
Not only was he mayor for life
I also considered him a genuine friend

To publicly honor his memory
With this poem, I start
Marion Barry made some mistakes
But feared God and had a good heart

Simply

A poem called, For Real – Not All
Is another, I recently wrote
Yet, as I analyze the situation
I write now to further make a note

All cops aren't bad
This I know for a fact
But, among those who are crooked
Some are also black

For a racist white cop to do us dirty
Isn't hard to believe
But, some black cops will do us dirty too
By no means be deceived

They'll do it for money or promotion
From integrity they are far apart
No doubt possessed by a demon
Self-ambition has enslaved their hearts

This truth isn't easy to accept
To ignore it indeed I tried
It's ridiculous to pretend
Impossible to be denied

Let us all appreciate good cops
And sing the most accurate version of the song
Although, racism is a significant component
It's simply about right and wrong

Psalm 106:3
Proverbs 11:3

Just As Good

He is disliked because of character defects
Like us, all he has he shares
Yet, many make excuses to hate on him
And safe to say, he doesn't care

Straight out of high school
He was drafted into the NBA
At the age of 36 and after two severe injuries
He still requires a double team when he plays

On the court, they call him "Black Mamba"
The "Trey," he continues to consistently drop
Still fast breaking and dunking
He beats people off the dribble then stops and pops

Recently, he surpassed M.J. on the scoring list
An incredible feat for sure
Only two other players in the history of the league
Have scored more

By now, it's obvious, I'm one of his fans
A fact I will not deny
I think he's better than Michael Jordan
The following will explain why

Kobe didn't start when he first got drafted
Himself, he still had to find
For the first two years of his pro career
He didn't get a lot of playing time

When he did begin to excel
His haters want to ignore the fact
Kobe's scoring average would have been much higher
But he shared the ball with Shaq

(CONTINUED FROM PREVIOUS PAGE)

Michael Jordan was the real deal
And to accept that we all should
It's hard to say Kobe is better
But, for a fact, he is just as good

Good Husband – Good Dad

Three days ago, I turned 46
By God's mercy without a doubt
Yet, I haven't produced any children
Or at least none that I know about

As well, I've never been married
Because self-destruction prioritize my life
Now, I'm back on the right track
And I want to be a father, also yearn for a God fearing wife

Needless to say, I'm at war with impatience
Literal combat with frustration
My immature choices are only to blame
No excuses or exaggeration

For the future, I'm optimistic
If the Lord is willing, I'll soon get engaged
Besides perfect health, I have a lot of potential
And even look younger than my age

God has kept me with favor I don't deserve
Because of this I refuse to be sad
For sure, I'll be a good husband
And to my offspring, a good dad

Ephesians 5:22-33
Ephesians 6:4
Colossians 3:18-21

Asking For Trouble

Christmas has been tainted
Its true meaning must be redeemed
The introduction of the myth of Santa Claus
Is one of the devil's well devised schemes

Instead of bringing the joy that it should
For many, Christmas causes nothing but stress
People waste money they can't afford to spend
And end up in a financial mess

It is really a shame
No doubt this fact the Lord does despise
Adults think it is cute to mislead children
And fill their heads with lies

Santa actually stands for Satan
The father of confusion invented this story
Santa Claus is a part of Satan's plan
To deprive Jesus of His glory

Sad to say, this matter is getting out of control
If you fear God you know it's not funny
Christmas now separates families and ruins friendships
It has become all about money

Please stop misleading children
Cease this deception on the double
Promoting this myth is supporting Satan
From Jesus you're asking for trouble

Hebrews 4:12-13

About The Author

James Daniel Johnson was born in Florence, South Carolina. He currently resides in the District of Columbia.

Accept It & Grow is Mr. Johnson's third book. His first, *Internal Reflections – It Is What It Is*, and second *This Will Make Ya Think*, are collections of poems about the adversities Mr. Johnson has faced, his Christian faith, and his relationships with family and friends.

About his life, Mr. Johnson says:

I have overcome childhood abuse, drug addiction, and alcoholism. The devil desires to destroy God's purpose for my life. Needless to say, the Lord will not allow that to happen. Amen.

Please check out Mr. Johnson's website:

www.danieldapoet.com

Made in the USA
Columbia, SC
27 May 2017